ANIMAL
BEHAVIOR

First edition for the United States, Canada,
and the Philippines published 1992
by Barron's Educational Series, Inc.

© Copyright by Aladdin Books, Ltd 1992

Design David West Children's Book Design
Illustrations Kate Taylor
Text Anita Ganeri
Picture research Emma Krikler

Created and designed by
N.W. Books
28 Percy Street
London W1P 9FF

All inquiries should be addressed to:
Barron's Educational Series, Inc.
250 Wireless Boulevard
Hauppauge, NY 11788

International Standard Book No. 0-8120-6301-5

Library of Congress Catalog Card No. 91-34184

Library of Congress Cataloging-in-Publication Data

Ganeri, Anita. 1961-
Animal behaviour / by Anita Ganeri : illustrated by Kate Taylor--1st ed.
p.   cm. -- (Questions and answers about--)
Summary: Presents information, in question-and-answer format,
about some of the common and uncommon aspects of animal behaviour.
ISBN 0-8120-6301-5
1. Animal behaviour--Miscellanea--Juvenile literature.
[1. Animals -- Habits and behaviour. 2. Questions and answers.]
I. Taylor, Kate, ill. II. Title. III. Series.
QL751.5.G36   1992
591.51 -- dc20   91-34184   CIP   AC

Printed in Belgium
2345   0987654321

QUESTIONS AND ANSWERS ABOUT
ANIMAL BEHAVIOR

Barron's

How do animals behave?

We behave in lots of different ways. We know how to do some things automatically. But we have to learn how to do other things. Most other animals behave instinctively. This means they automatically know how to do some things. But, just like us, some skills have to be learned. This book will help you learn more about the many ways in which animals behave, including some weird and wonderful activities – such as taking hot baths and changing color.

Which animals learn quickly?

Chimpanzees, apes, and monkeys all learn quickly. A rhesus monkey in Australia learned to drive a tractor. A gorilla called Koko learned how to use a camera.

8

Which is the smartest animal?

Scientists think that chimpanzees may be the smartest animals. They learn to do things very quickly. Some chimps have learned human sign language. They even use it to talk to each other. Chimps like to play games, but they can also solve problems.

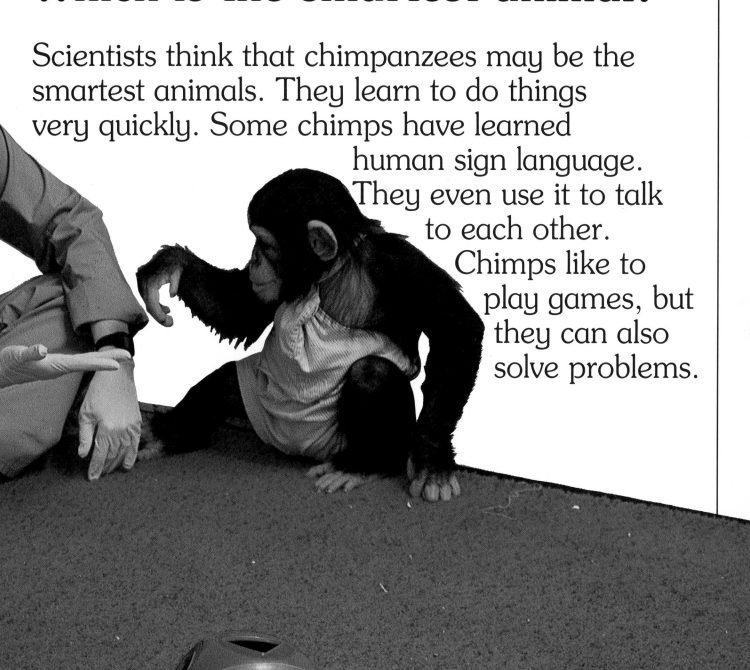

How do lion cubs learn to hunt?

A good way of learning how to do things is by playing games. Lion cubs learn hunting skills by playing with their mother's tail! They pounce on the twitching black hair at the end of her tail. When they are grown up, they have to use these same skills to kill prey.

How do baby otters learn to fish?

Baby otters practice their underwater hunting skills with a dead fish! Their mother brings a fish back to the otters' pond and puts it in the water. The babies dive and chase after it.

Why do animals hibernate in winter?

In winter, it is often very cold and there is very little food available. Therefore, some animals spend the winter in a deep sleep. This deep sleep is called hibernation. Bats, dormice, and bears all hibernate in winter.

Which animals hibernate in summer?

In the desert, it is very hot and dry in summer. The Mojave squirrel stays cool by sleeping in its underground burrow for days. Some snails, crocodiles, fish, and snakes also hibernate in summer.

Why do animals migrate?

In winter, many birds, bats, and butterflies travel to warmer places where there is more food. In September, monarch butterflies fly about 2,500 miles (4,000 kilometers) from northern Canada to California and Mexico in the south.

How do they find their way?

No one is sure how animals find their way on their journeys. Some birds use landmarks such as mountains and valleys to guide them. Others use the sun and stars. Some seem to have a built-in compass. They know automatically where to go.

15

How do salmon find the right river?

Every year, thousands of salmon leave the sea and swim back upriver to lay their eggs. Amazingly, they find their way to the exact spot in the river where they were born. They do this by taste. Each river tastes slightly different. The taste is created by chemicals in the water.

Which animals sometimes get lost?

Adelie penguins walk over 200 miles (300 kilometers) to get to their breeding grounds. The penguins use the sun to guide them. If the sun is hidden by clouds, the penguins sometimes get lost.

How do moles "see" underground?

Because moles live underground, they don't need very good eyesight. In fact, they can only see the difference between light and dark. They find their way around by smell and by feeling with the bristles on their cheeks.

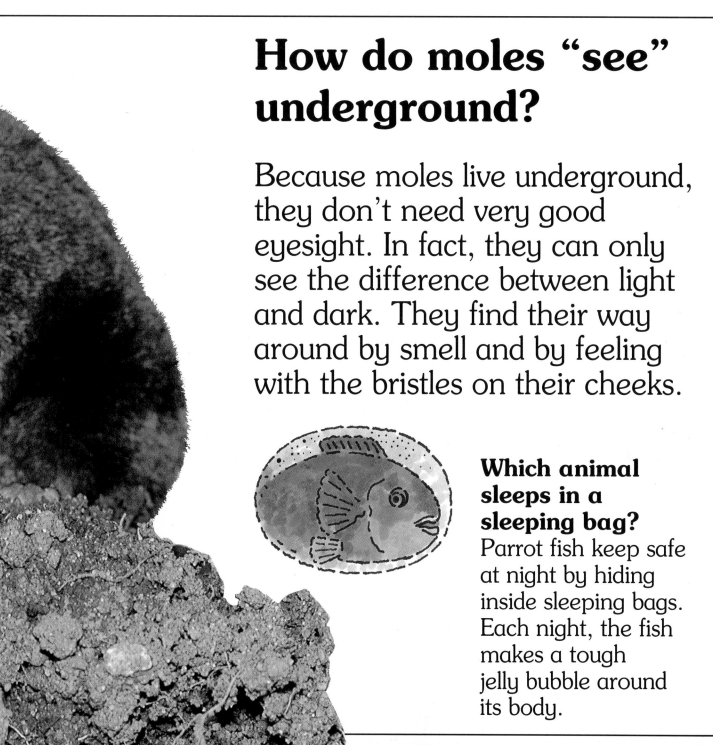

Which animal sleeps in a sleeping bag?
Parrot fish keep safe at night by hiding inside sleeping bags. Each night, the fish makes a tough jelly bubble around its body.

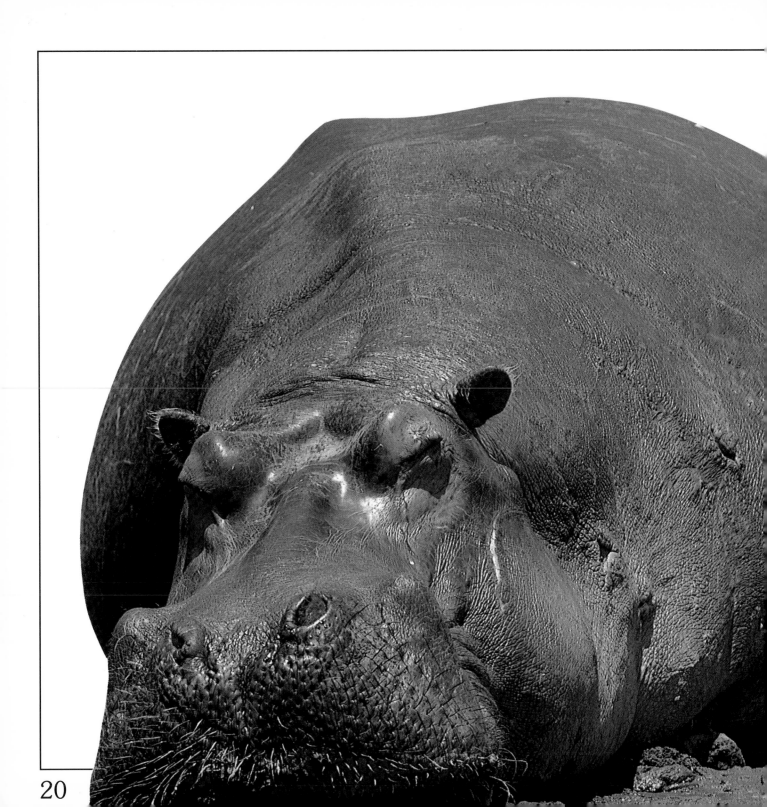

Why do hippos wallow in the mud?

Hippos live near rivers and swamps in Africa. They spend most of the day in the water, or even underwater. Hippos love to roll around in the mud along the river bank. This helps to keep them cool. It also helps soothe itchy insect stings and bites on the hippo's skin.

Which animals take hot baths?
Macaque monkeys live in the cold mountains of Japan. There are lots of warm springs there which the monkeys bathe in to keep warm.

Why do snakes shed their skin?

Snakes have to change their skin several times a year. This is called sloughing. The snake needs a new skin because the old skin gets worn out as the snake slithers along the ground. Snakes crawl out of their old skin head first, leaving the entire old skin behind.

Why do fireflies glow?

Fireflies are actually beetles. Their bodies contain special chemicals that produce light. Fireflies come out at night. They flash their lights on and off to send signals to other fireflies.

23

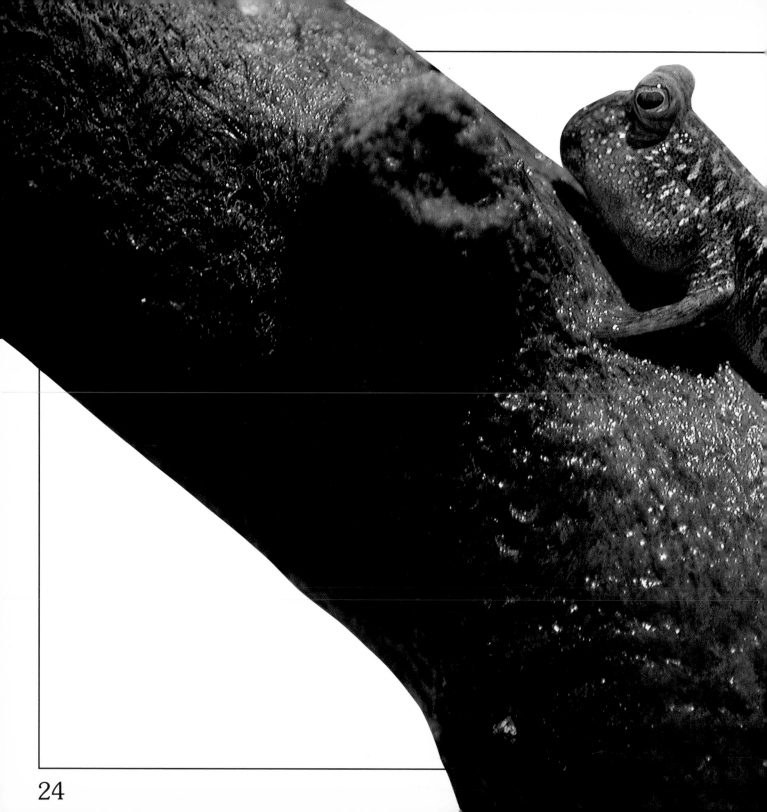

Which fish climb trees?

Mudskippers are fish that live in tropical swamps. They can live in and out of the water. They spend most of their time out of the water looking for food in the mud.

To escape from danger, mudskippers flick their bodies and shoot across the mud. Some can even climb trees. They have special sucker-like fins to grip the tree trunks.

Why do oysters make pearls?

Oysters sometimes get tiny objects inside their shells. To prevent irritations they cover them with layers of calcium carbonate. This forms a pearl.

How do moray eels get their teeth cleaned?

Moray eels are long, snake-like fish that live on coral reefs. If scraps of food get stuck in their teeth, the eels line up at a special cleaning station on the reef. Here, little cleaner fish swim inside their mouths and clean their teeth!

Why do jays use ants as cleaners?

Ants produce a type of acid that kills lice. Jays rub ants over their feathers to get rid of lice.

How does a baby bird recognize its mother?

When baby birds hatch, they automatically follow the first large thing they see. This is usually their mother. They follow her around and copy what she does. But if the first thing they see is a person or even an object, they will accept this as their mother.

How does a chameleon know when to change color?

Chameleons change color to blend in with their surroundings. They have special pigments in their skin that change automatically when the color of the background changes.

Index

Photographs

Cover and pages 6, 8-9, 10-11, 14-15, 18-19, 22-23, 24-25 and 26- 27: Bruce Coleman Limited; pages 12-13: Survival Anglia Photo Library; pages 16-17 and 20-21: Planet Earth Pictures; pages 28- 29: J. Allan Cash Photo Library.